Life is Ibiza

LIFE IS

IBI

PEOPLE
HOUSES
LIFE

ZA

LANNOO

Life is Ibiza

Only the best is good enough for the large minority who live life with sensitivity and to whom beauty is the universal language.

Ibiza Love

My love for Ibiza knows no bounds, as should be abundantly clear from my second book about this, my beloved island. On this occasion, I take you on a tour of the island's prettiest houses, introducing you to some inspiring kindred souls that have grown permanent roots on the island. Everyone needs a little Ibiza in their life, if only by leafing through this book and letting oneself be carried away to that place where the sun always shines and people live in tune with nature.

Ibiza has been a part of my life for thirty-five years; it is my second home and the place where I would spend my school holidays as a child. I know Benirras beach from the hippies that would gather there at dusk to make music, Es Cavallet beach I remember as the nude beach with one big beach cabine, where you could eat tasty fish, and in the eighties my parents would go partying in the Ku (now the Privilege), where you could watch dancers performing on stage in the nude and engage in some quite naughty activity yourself, too. Everything for love.

If you had to summarise Ibiza in a single word, to me it would be *CONTRAST*. (Boho-chic) hippies and the internationally rich and famous live side by side. Blakstad *fincas* and unique modern houses stand in sharp contrast. But anything goes, and every house blends into the island's landscape in its own unique way. A concept that kept coming up when I was interviewing people was freedom. Freedom to be whoever you want to be, to live and let live. Too good to be true? See for yourself in this fantastic book that I poured my heart and soul into.

LOVE
Anne

Contents

Houses

People

THIS IS IBIZA

'I'd love to stay on this island of madness.' — Grace Jones

THIS IS IBIZA

Ever since the thirties and particularly the sixties, Ibiza has drawn numerous creative people, artists, free birds, hippies, and cult figures like a magnet. And there's a reason. It's not just the breath-taking beauty of its unspoiled natural surroundings and sea; its attraction goes deeper. This cosmopolitan island has a unique identity that stands out for its tolerance, kindred souls, and the unconventional. In the nineties, foreigners started building villas on a large scale with views of the sea. Many cult figures and jet-setters—film stars, models, fashion designers, sports celebrities, etc.—have meanwhile found a spot here, enjoying their freedom and anonymity. Ibiza's magic is evident in the surprising dream houses you find all over the island and in its multitude of architectural styles, ranging from authentic Ibiza style to modern, usually minimalist architecture.

NATURE

Ibiza has different areas that are of special interest because of their ecological value and natural beauty. The two most prominent ones are the Ses Salines Natural Park and Es Vedrà, the lone rock in the sea. Ses Salines is located between the south of Ibiza and north of Formentera. It has a surface area of 1,786.52 terrestrial and 13,661.80 marine hectares. This park comprises a large variety of environments with different ecological traits: the beaches, salt ponds, dunes, Sabine trees, cliffs, and rocky coastline.

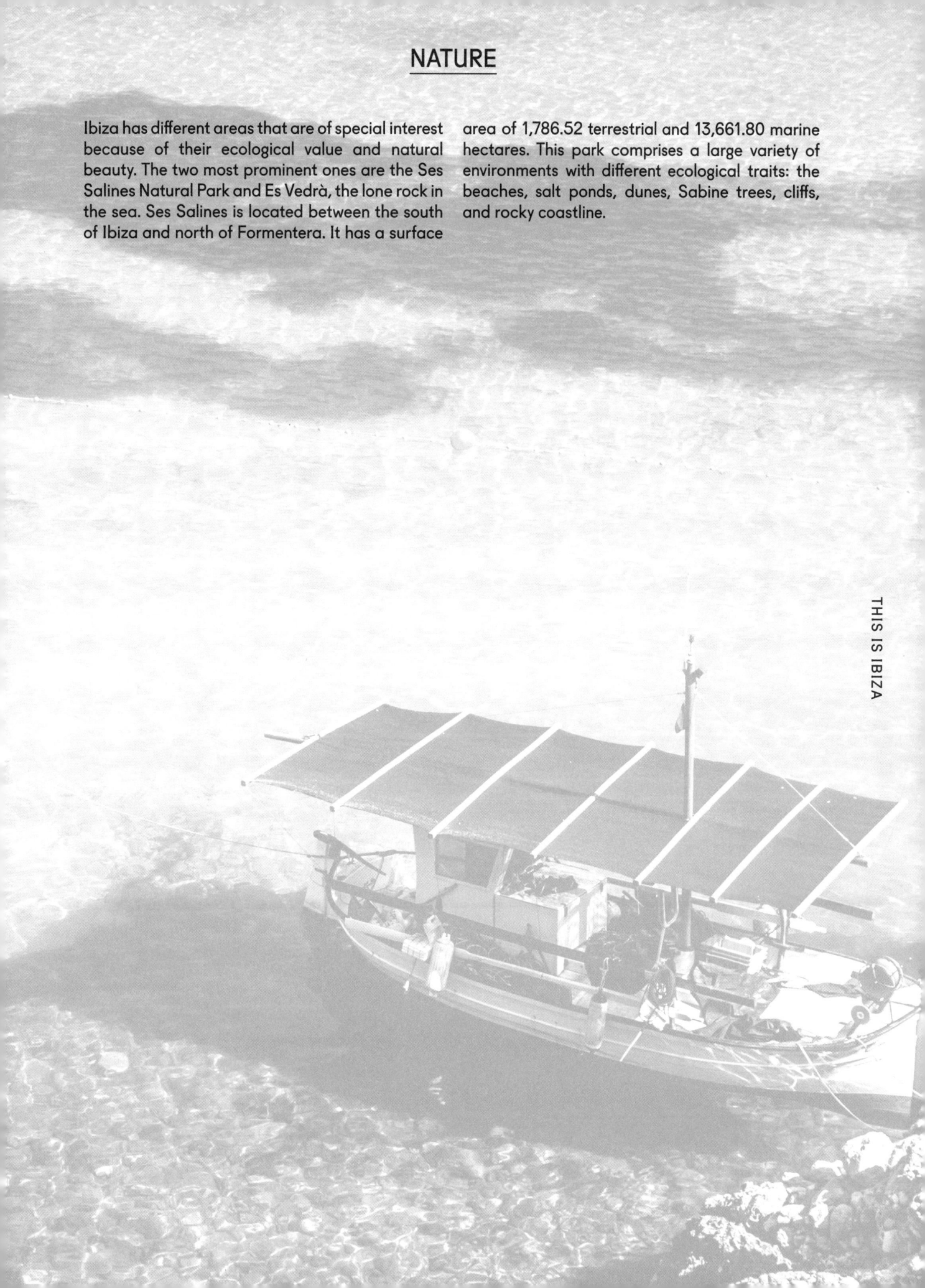

ES VEDRA

The mythical rock is often the first thing mentioned when people speak of Ibiza. Located in the southwest, this is—just like the salt flats—a natural park, one that is some 413 metres high and consists predominantly of Mesozoic limestone. It contains such high mineral and metal concentrations that the island is the third most magnetic place on earth! When boats come too close to the island, their compasses can start malfunctioning, and sensitive people can even feel the radiation. For these reasons you will almost never see fishing boats near Es Vedra. Popular wisdom has it that people seeking healing can accelerate the process by touching the rock.

Of course, such a mythical place comes with its own collection of stories and popular myths: UFOs have supposedly been sighted on the rock, and a bright, white light also regularly makes an appearance. An unwritten law among locals says that no one is to take tourists to Es Vedra; the risk of destruction by excess tourism is too high. You can still get there by private boat, of course, and you are supposed to take care to preserve the place.

Es Vedra was also once the original name for the whole of Ibiza. As the island's occupants changed, so did its name, until it eventually and definitively became Ibiza!

SAL DE IBIZA

Sal de Ibiza, the salt from Ibiza, has been harvested in the saline fields on the Balearic island of Ibiza for over 2.700 years. The island's inhabitants have always been very proud of the premium quality of their marine salt, regarded as one of the best of its kind. The exquisite Sal de Ibiza is exclusively harvested in the Nature reserve 'Parc Natural de ses Salines d'Eivissa', proclaimed a UNESCO World Heritage Site in 1999. The symbiosis of traditional craftsmanship, plentiful sun and light winds, creates this wholly natural sea-salt, which is obtained solely by the natural evaporation of seawater. It contains no additives or preservatives, nor does it undergo any form of refinement other than slow drying under the sun and gentle grinding in ancient stone mills, enabling Sal de Ibiza to retain its more than eighty vital minerals and trace-elements detectable in seawater.

FOLK & TRADITION

You might think that the massive influx of foreigners and the combination of cultures that the island represents would have weakened Ibizan traditions, but that has not been the case. To the contrary, in fact: they have contributed to the preservation and even enhancement of the local culture and traditions. The Ibizan people take refuge in their identity and culture, and they love sharing them.

BALL PAGÈS

In Ibiza, craftsmen find someone whom they can pass their knowledge and skills on to, and popular songs are transmitted from grandparents to grandchildren. The *ball pagès*, the traditional peasant dance on the island, goes back hundreds, maybe thousands, of years. You can watch the *ball pagès* being performed in the old communal wells or in front of the church anytime there is a celebration. This tradition is truly very important for the Ibizan people. Historical research has shown that these dances, with a choreography that repeats number eight's circles and figures, are ancient in origin. Worthy of note is the presence of women in the dances: their jewels, called *emprendadas*, are a joy for the eye. In the *ball pagès*, men invite women to dance with a strong click on their castanets.

ANCIENT CITY

The city of Eivissa looks out towards the sea and the acropolis. The fortress of Dalt Vila (the old city of Ibiza) is integrated into the daily life of its people, from breakfast to shopping to drinks, and is the incomparable setting of the island"s great artistic, social and cultural events. The Renaissance wall is constituted by seven bastions. Sant Pere, also called Es Portal Nou, is one of the entrances to the site, next to the Reina Sofia park. Here the soldiers were positioned to face the enemies. Today it is the incomparable scene of outdoor concerts.

Another gateway to Dalt Vila is the Portal de ses Taules, where the spectacular fortress courtyard is located, and the Plaça de Vila, full of charming restaurants, art galleries, and craft shops, surrounded by a framework of stone that breathes history through all its cracks.

The construction of the Renaissance wall of Eivissa was part of the plan to modernise the coastal defences of the Mediterranean, promoted by Charles I and Philip II to maintain and defend the territories of the Spanish Crown in a time of war with France and the Ottoman Empire.

When the Turkish and Berber pirates waned and the island ceased to be the target of new attacks, the acropolis stood for posterity as a testimony of that time, and today is a UNESCO World Heritage Site. This international award acknowledges its historical, cultural, and architectural value. It is the best preserved piece of coastline in the whole Mediterranean area. The Dalt Vila acropolis is surrounded by narrow alleys and monuments such as the castle and the cathedral. These days it is the stage for concerts, cultural activities, exhibitions and more.

PARTY

The Ibizan way of life has always inspired and attracted many people: from the creative to the eccentric, they all feel at home and give their talents a free rein. Musical geniuses have found a platform in the best music temples on earth, where they can freely experiment and start new trends. Summer after summer, music professionals from all over the world gather here. Pacha, Amnesia, DC10, and Privilege were the first temples of music and they still exist because they are reputed to be among the best discotheques on earth. Every week partygoers can don different costumes and participate in the famous themed parties, with the hippy theme no doubt being the most important one. Legendary parties enhanced with audiovisual effects, go-go dancers on stage, performances, and unprecedented innovation. The party continues, season after season.

The high values of tolerance, generosity, and love make Ibiza the legend it is. Pink Floyd were inspired there, the Bee Gees used to rehearse in San Antonio, and Cat Stevens sang his *Moonshadow* in the port. Eric Clapton and Bob Marley performed in Ibiza, and George Michael recorded his hit song *Tropicana* here.

Ibiza has always been a refuge for intellectuals, artists, hedonists, and nonconformists. At the end of the seventies Ibiza's own particular music style was born, the *Balearic Beat*, which has survived to this day. The nineties saw electronic music invading the island, taking over the best parties with the best DJs in the world.

BLAKSTAD & FINCA

Ibiza is not only modern villas. The traditional *finca* style building can be seen cropping up all over the island. The people from Ibiza designed their own house structure, the peasant house, that still stands today against the modern world. They are century-long constructions considered as the origin of well-established customs, such as meeting on the traditional porxo or porch. Ibiza's landscape is dotted with the most beautiful whitewashed houses made out of different-size cubes that grow with new spaces as the family grows. They are always facing the sun. The old peasant houses are passed down from generation to generation, and renovations are made while trying to respect traditional architecture.

THE FINCA

Ibiza's timeless and sober architecture is character-ised by a succession of complementary functional, cubist modules that can be adapted to the needs of the family.

This type of architecture has many striking features. The way the houses are placed (taking into account the sun's position so as to avoid overheating), spread out, and integrated into the landscape; the use of local materials; the metre-thick, whitewashed walls; the absence of decorative elements; the flat roofs; the small windows; the wooden-beam ceilings ... The original *finca* had much of a small fort, providing protection against enemies and the summer heat.
Though archaic, Ibizan architecture still manages to surprise even the most modern-minded. It is eco-logically durable and extremely well adapted to the climate. Made of clay and lime, Ibizan houses are cool in the summer and warm in winter.
The *fincas*, scattered all over the island, are oases of peace and tranquillity. Ibiza's plain and function-al *finca* clearly shows more similarity with Moorish mansions than with the houses on its sister islands of Mallorca and Menorca, which have undergone Catalan and Castilian influences.
Modern architects set to work with this. They usual-ly stayed true to the modular structure around the porxo (portal) and the thick, whitewashed walls, while making serious modifications in response to contemporary needs.

THE INFLUENCE OF ROLPH BLAKSTAD

After years of research, Canadian Rolph Blakstad brought a new style of architecture to Ibiza, a modern version of the Ibizan building style still heavily influenced by the original. In fact, he was the first to reinterpret the traditional Ibizan *finca* or renovate it according to the rules.
As a modern minimalist, Blakstad tried to main-tain traditional methods, techniques, and building materials, but at the same time his designs featured spacious, airy rooms, high windows, and big terraces and pergolas. He was also a real trend-setter with his brickwork kitchen cabinets with typical rough, wooden doors, something widely copied and imitat-ed by many architects nowadays.
The emphasis lies on minimalist simplicity, symmetri-cal beauty, and limited visual impact on the natural and historical Ibizan landscape.
Blakstad imitators are still very active on the island and enjoy great popularity among the internation-al community that are looking for charming villas. Blakstad has been known for his traditional *finca* building style for the past 50 years.

NOSTRADAMUS

One of the weird theories about Ibiza was authored by Nostradamus, who said that it will be the only place on earth left standing in case of a nuclear war. As he famously put it: 'Ibiza will be Earth's final refuge after the final verdict.' In these times of war and extreme terrorism, this may provide some welcome peace of mind.

FOOD

Ibiza lures you with its heavenly climate, people, landscapes, and the best gastronomy on the beach, in historical places, in the countryside, or beneath a star-filled sky.

Find pleasure in eating natural products at their perfect point of ripeness and experience a sense of peace and freedom while savouring a dish of fresh tuna, sea bass, or squid.

Mix the pleasures of good food and traditions: traditional dishes are the best.

- *Sofrit pagès: sofrit pagès* is an Ibizan dish of gently spiced pork, lamb, and chicken, with delicious local *sobresada* and *butifarra* sausages, whole sweet garlics, peppers, and potatoes, all vaporised in their own rich juices and sautéed with cinnamon, parsley, and saffron.
- *Guisat de peix*: a dish with fish, potatoes, local ingredients, and sometimes almonds.
- *Greixonera*: something similar to a bread pudding.
- *Flaó*: the island's unique round cheesecake, made with fresh cheese—goat or sheep—and spearmint leaves.

Let yourself get carried away by the local wines (Ibizan wines are made and produced in areas of San Mateu, Buscastell, and Sant Josep), and be sure to taste the olive oil and peasant bread, delicacies that can be found on every table. They accompany the magical moment in which eating is the equivalent of taking care of yourself, learning new things, sharing, and smiling.

Hierbas de Ibiza is a very popular drink in Ibiza and is part of the tradition of many households that have always made them at home. Each family follows its own recipe, which, in many occasions, is secret. *Hierbas* de Ibiza is made using local herbs: rosemary, thyme, mint, peppermint, juniper, sage, fennel, lavender, and lemon- and orange-tree leaves.

Houses

People

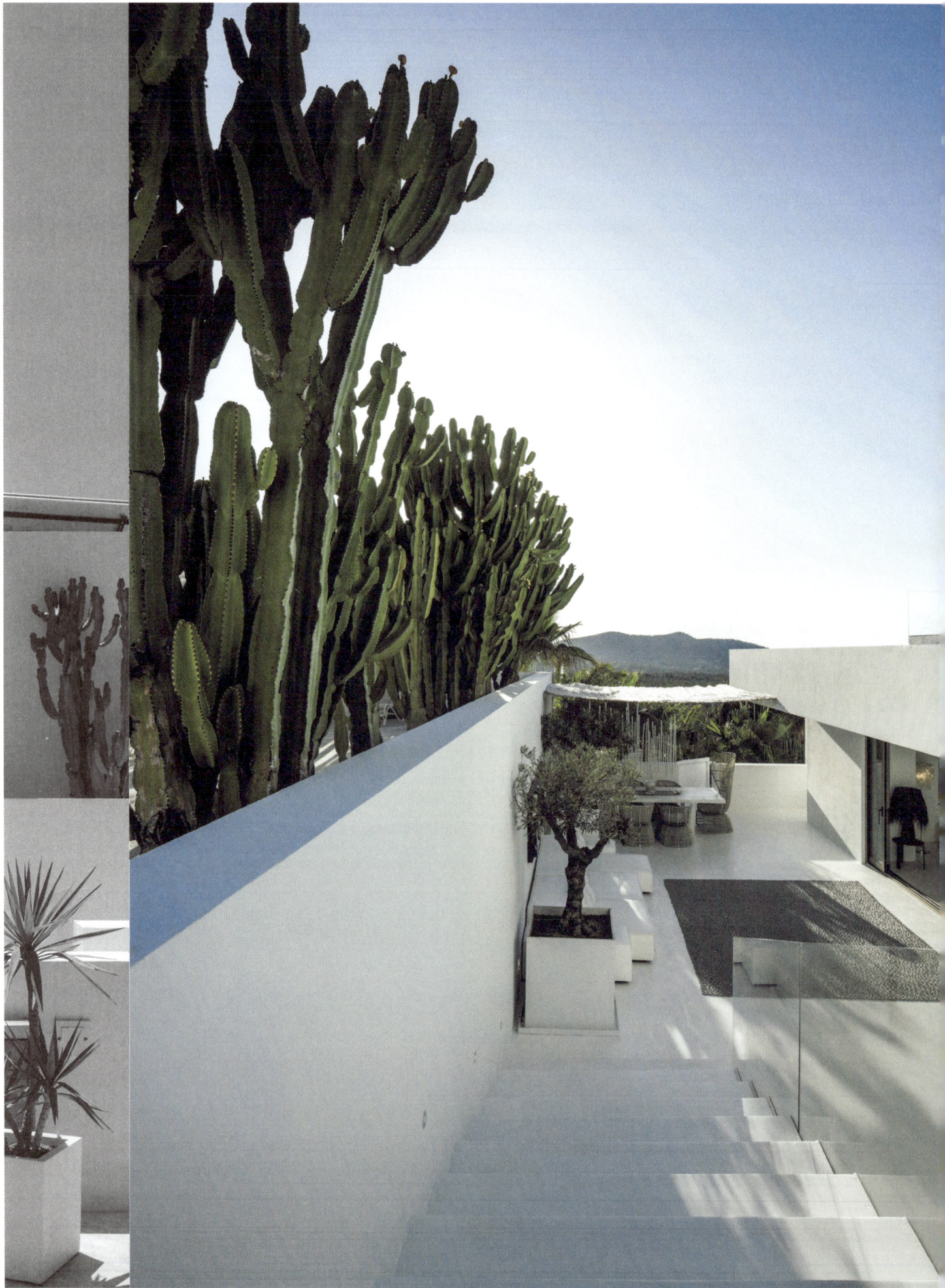

Villa Mediterraneo

Secret location

The villa looks discreet on the outside; it's on the inside where its posh side gains more prominence. Located on a hill overlooking the sea, the white walls stand in stark contrast to the azure sea. The large windows draw nature and light inside. The minimalist decor interacts harmoniously with the structure and colours of the house. The ceilings in the living area are covered with thousands of small mirrors that reflect light and images in all directions: a regular work of art. Almost all the furniture is white, blending with the rest of the house and letting its architecture express itself. The revolving stairs look decidedly futuristic and take you up to the rooftop level.

No wonder that this luxury villa cost a fortune: it was built by Metroarea, an architectural firm from Trieste, Italy, who designed it taking into consideration six design parameters: perspective, the possibility of accessing the roofs, organic lines, functions, the hilliness of the area, and the inner courtyards.

HOUSES

← Metroarea, an architectural firm from Trieste, Italy, who designed this house took into consideration six design parameters: perspective, the possibility of accessing the roofs, organic lines, functions, the hilliness of the area, and the inner courtyards.

→ The ceilings in the living area are covered with thousands of small mirrors that reflect light and images in all directions: a regular work of art.

63

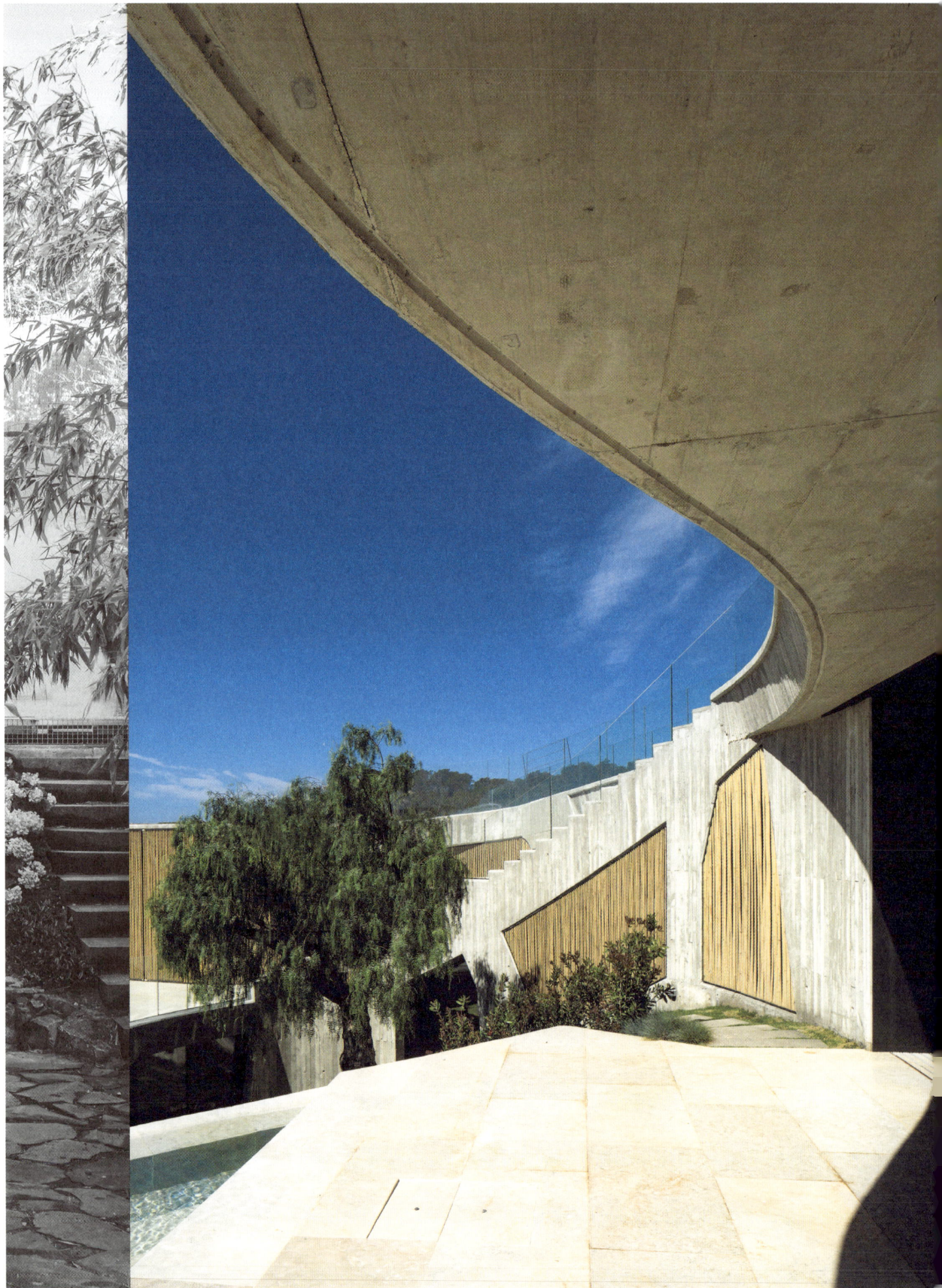

Hidden Treasure

Secret location

The fusion of architecture with Mediterranean culture and nature turns this house into a unique sample of human ingenuity, including that of philosopher and architect Rudolf Steiner, whose work is an invitation to distance oneself from Euclidean design and to construct in a more expressive way.

Nature is actively drawn into this 1,600-square-metre house by the large windows surrounded by hanging gardens, canopies, bamboo shutters, and rough natural stone. The patio is the nerve centre of a complex network of corridors and paths that criss-cross the house. Rain water is gathered by a real impluvium and collected in a cistern, which directs any excess water to a decorative waterfall. A small creek connects the two swimming pools.

The complex has three different construction levels connected by curved paths and stairs. The ground floor contains the master suite with adjoining living room and wardrobe, while the other wing of the building houses six guest rooms and the main pool. The first floor has a living room which you enter through an imposing fifteen-metre-long sliding door. The dining room, kitchen, spa, gym, and secondary external pool are all part of the first floor. The second floor features a large Belvedere living room.

The shape of the villa follows the ground's natural slope, creating the impression that it hugs the terrain in perfect harmony, like a kind of amphitheatre surrounded by nature. The materials used are all very simple, irregular board-formed concrete and drywall. This highlights the builders' desire to make the complex look more alternative and not too blingy. The result is an informal, inviting house that has a strong connection with the island while at the same time following the rules of architects such as Busiri Vici, Couelle, and Vietti.

HOUSES

← The shape of the villa follows the ground's natural slope, creating the impression that it hugs the terrain in perfect harmony, like a kind of amphitheatre surrounded by nature.

The fusion of architecture with Mediterranean culture and nature turns this house into a unique sample of human ingenuity.

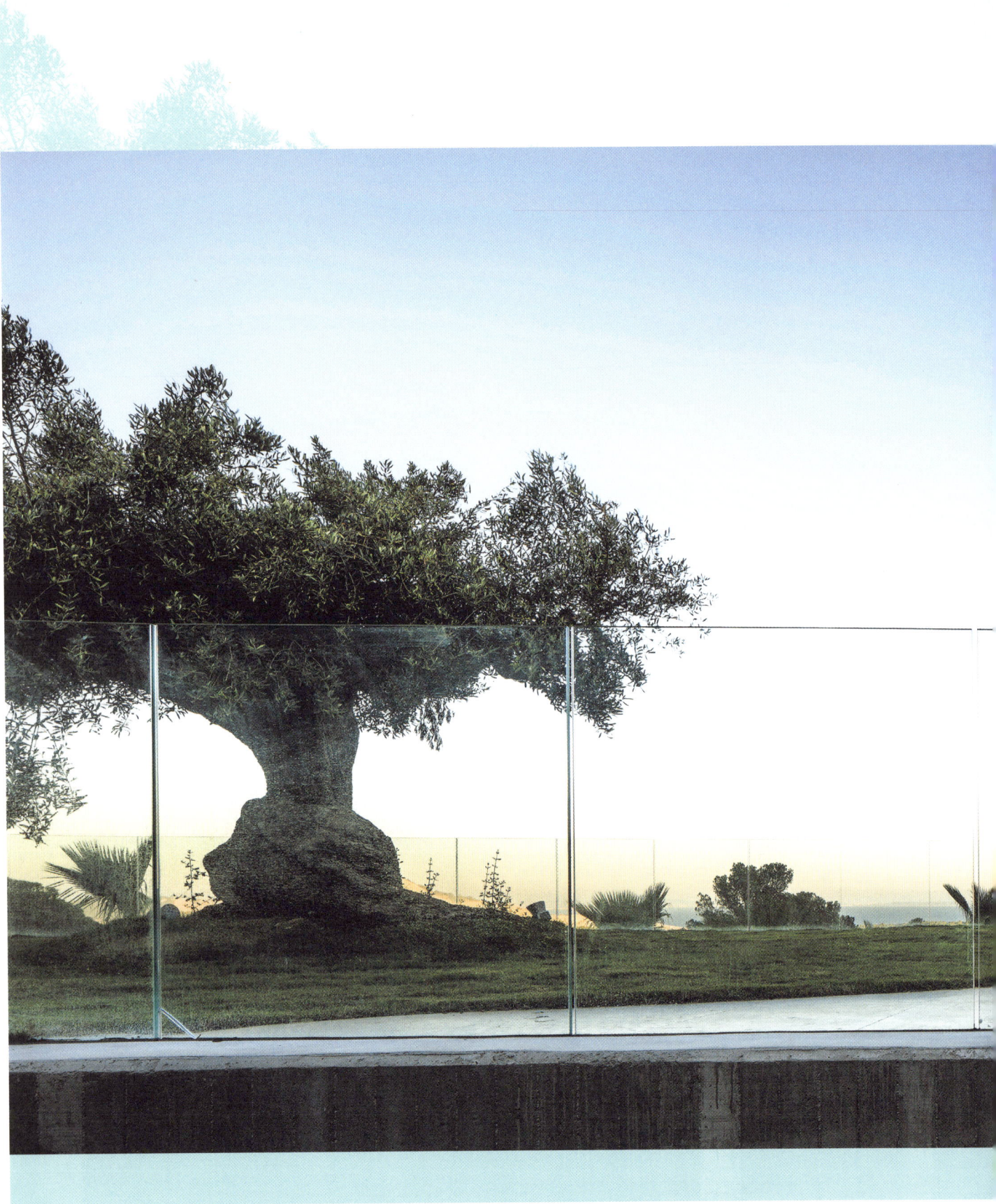

↓ Nature is actively drawn into this 1,600-square-metre house by the large windows surrounded by hanging gardens, canopies, bamboo shutters, and rough natural stone.

Saba Rahbar

HOLISTIC CHEF
FOR TREEHOUSE KITCHEN

I-D
--------------------- ——— Age: 28 years
--------------------- ——— Has been living in Ibiza for a year.
--------------------- ——— Lives in San Carlos.
--------------------- ——— Instagram: @treehouseibiza

What's your story? How did you end up in Ibiza? ——— I visited the island for the first time seven years ago after much convincing. You see, I had this totally different view of the island. I spent four days in the north and this completely changed my perception of what the island has to offer. After those four days, my life was never the same: my whole mind-set about life and about where and how I wanted to live had changed. After living in Qatar and London for a couple of years, I decided to take a risk and a year ago I moved here. I didn't know many people before moving. However, I was very fortunate to quickly connect with such warm and welcoming residents. I have always had a catering business, so I was able to continue living my passion in Ibiza. Now I organise workshops on plant based cooking, provide catering services for retreats, organise pop-up lunches in organic farms, and I am in the process of developing a product line using Ibizan almonds. Life is good here.

What is it about the island that attracts you most? ——— It's more of a feeling than anything concrete: there is this strong feeling of love that is for me really predominant. I'm originally from Iran, but was born in Canada, grew up between Dubai and the UK and went to university in Paris. So for me home has always been a strange concept. Even before I lived here, I really felt very much at home; it felt familiar. I had this bond with the earth.

How do you fill in your days? ——— I get up at seven every day and start my morning meditation and stretching exercises. Then I go for a long walk with my dog in the countryside. In the morning I usually do my computer work and bookkeeping, etc. At noon I prepare a healthy lunch. In the afternoon I disappear into my kitchen and start experimenting with recipes and working on my own cookbook. Any fresh products I need I get from the market and from local farmers. During the summer months I try to go to the beach every day, the salt water recharges me.

What is your favourite spot in Ibiza? ——— There's a secret cove tucked away and a big boulder with crystals and quartz in it; it's beautiful. To me it's like a place of pilgrimage where I can find myself or take my closest girlfriends. Take some homemade food for a picnic and somehow time stops existing!

Where would you be living if Ibiza didn't exist? ——— My best friend is from Maui, I have visited her there and got a similar feeling to the one I have in Ibiza.

--------------------- Remote, rural setting
--------------------- A waterfront infinity pool
--------------------- Contrasts of rough wood and sleek lines
--------------------- *Mirador* views

87

Casa Alegre

Porroig

When Fernando de Castro of Ark International Studio started designing this house, he knew he would take the sea as his central starting point. All lines run parallel to the sea, creating the impression in some rooms that you are actually out at sea. All bedrooms offer sea views, and you feel like you can just roll out of your bed into the sea. The magnificent portal with wooden beams (from the Netherlands) looks out over the infinity pool that transitions into the sea, surrounded by a garden that descends to the turquoise water

of the bay below. On the other side we find enormous glass spaces that blend in with the landscape. This Mediterranean house's DNA is clearly courtesy of Ark International Studio.

The ground floor houses all the living spaces, the kitchen, the terraces, and the sixty-metre-long swimming pool. On the first floor we find the sleeping quarters and bathrooms.

The exterior spaces were designed to be used as true living spaces, providing the house's inhabitants and guests a homely feeling while spending summer evenings on the terrace. Large floor-to-ceiling glass panes let the landscape and light flow into the house. The panes slide on integrated rails, making it possible to reconfigure the spaces.

The central chair is by Jaser Morrison for Vitra, the Lounge Chair & Ottoman by Charles & Ray Eames for Vitra. The side tables come from Gunni & Trentino, the shop (with its own label) where most of the house's furniture was purchased.

The swimming pool runs even with the house, forming a parallel line with the horizon. The exterior furniture is by the well-known brand of Kettal.

→ All lines run parallel to the sea,
creating the impression in some
rooms that you are actually out at sea.

89

→ The exterior spaces were designed to be used as true
living spaces, providing the house's inhabitants and
guests a homely feeling.

93

---------------------- Lounge terrace with glittering sea views
---------------------- Pool with a shallow end
---------------------- Inside is outside is inside
---------------------- Iconic design furniture

97

Casa Viddal & Rahola

Cala Salada

Victor Rahola and Jorge Vidal of Rahola Vidal Arquitectes collaborated with Catalan interior architect Marcos Catalan to build an imposing, bright landscape house. The basic materials jump out a lot: stone, concrete, sisal, and wicker are the elements with which the architects declare their love for the Ibizan landscape.

When someone builds a house on Ibiza, they particularly want to enjoy the beauty of the island's nature and its mild weather conditions which make it possible to live outdoors day and night. This idea was central in the design of this holiday home.

Architecturally, the house consists of two elongated blocks stacked one on top of the other, with special materials such as sisal and hemp softening the building's geometry. The top floor was conceived as a pavilion split in three and partly covered with sisal fibre and furnished with furniture that accentuates the horizontal flow. The ground floor—with its living room, three bedrooms, and playroom—was built around a stone and concrete walk-through veranda that crosses the whole house. The central axis of the ground floor is a big cork table designed by the interior architect himself.

The interior features furniture items such as the Tokyo chaise longue designed by Charlotte Perriand for Cassina, Miguel Milá's Cesta lamp for Santa & Cole, and modular chairs and coffee tables designed by Estudio Marcos Catalán.

On the sisal rug stands a Tokyo chaise longue designed by Charlotte Perriand for Cassina and a Cesta lamp made by Miguel Milá for Santa & Cole. The long wooden bench, made in iroko wood, is an Estudio Marcos Catalán design. Hemp rugs connect the furniture items with the elements of nature outside. The interior floors extend outside, where they automatically change purpose, becoming a terrace. From inside the elongated pool you can watch the sea glimmer in the distance.

↓ Stone, concrete, sisal, and wicker are the elements with which the architects declare their love for the Ibizan landscape.

→ Special materials such as sisal and hemp soften the building's geometry.

↓ Architecturally, the house consists of two elongated blocks stacked one on top of the other, with special materials such as sisal and hemp softening the building's geometry.

David Leppan

ENTREPRENEUR, ART COLLECTOR AND
OWNER OF LOS PATIOS IBIZA

I-D
-------------------- Age: 44 years
-------------------- Has been coming to Ibiza all his life.
-------------------- Lives in Roca Lisa.
-------------------- Instagram: @davidleppan

What's your story? How did you end up in Ibiza? —— My dad arrived here in 1974 and immediately fell in love with the island. He would visit regularly and one day took me along to his 'happy place on earth'. I remember standing on an Ibiza golf course as a child and being overwhelmed by this blissful feeling of belonging, a place that I connected with. A place where my senses were sharpened. Even while living in South Africa, I had this deep-rooted desire to live in Ibiza. And so it came to be that I moved here definitively, met my wife here, married, and became a father of three. My house in Ibiza is a home away from home. It is located on a rock in Roca Lisa. I can see the sun rise in the morning, the Island of Formentera and the green of the golf course from my bed. Heaven is a place on earth, and I'm definitely never ever leaving this place.

What is it about the island that attracts you most? —— For me, Ibiza is the most tolerant place on earth. Tolerance is there for anything that is genuine. As long as it is authentic, Ibiza will tolerate anything. It does not matter how crazy you are or how foolishly you dress, if you do it in an authentic way, it is fine.

How do you fill in your days? —— My bedroom offers me the best view possible of the sunrise. I want to see this every day of my life, so that's why I never close the curtains. No matter how tired I am, I get up with the first rays of the sun, take a dip in the swimming pool, and have breakfast next to the pool. Then I usually go to inspect the construction activities at the restaurant/private club I am opening; we have to be up and running by the summer of 2018. Then I have lunch at home, a siesta—I need it because I only sleep a few hours at night as I always get up at the break of dawn—and in the afternoon I do something with the kids. In the evening, I sometimes go to a restaurant but not very often. I turn in around one. It's late but it's a rhythm that works well on the island.

What is your favourite spot in Ibiza? —— My house is undoubtedly number one, but there's another place I like to be: at sea, in my boat, at the Es Vedra rock. You can see the sun go down there, and there's magic in the air. Sometimes, at the beginning of the season, I see dolphins there. By the summer they're gone, because of all the activity. Of course, I completely understand their departure. Off season, I like to go to Cala Bonita or Can Domo to enjoy the island's best food.

Where would you be living if Ibiza didn't exist? —— That's an impossible question, because I can't even imagine Ibiza not existing. I can't 'be' without Ibiza.

Can Uri

Around San José

This house belongs to Uri Fruchtmann, Annie Lennox's former husband, who made it his main residence. He did not furnish it in the usual Ibizan way, although the furniture and other objects blend well with the whole. The old *finca* was meticulously renovated under Uri's watchful eye, with absolute priority being given to authenticity. Everything revolves around antique furniture and objects: the Louis XIV chairs turn the fireplace into a cosy reading area, solid wooden blocks serve as side tables or commodes, and the bathtub is a hollowed-out piece of rock.

Notice how the bathroom was furnished as a living space complete with dining table, chair, and chandelier. The Panton chairs by Vitra, the only modern element in the house, give the terrace a pink touch.

The garden is divided into different levels, with each level or sublevel having its own function: reading, relaxing, swimming, or dreamily drifting off while you're looking out to sea. Plants are allowed to grow wild, lending the terraces some substance. The obligatory lavender spreads its heavenly fragrance throughout the garden.

HOUSES

The old *finca* was meticulously
renovated, with absolute priority
being given to authenticity.
Everything revolves around antique
furniture and objects.

The garden is divided into different levels, with each level or sublevel having its own function: reading, relaxing, swimming, or dreamily drifting off while you're looking out to sea.

---------------------- An eclectic whole
---------------------- Ibiza meets Morocco
---------------------- Landscaped gardens
---------------------- The terraced pool area is party perfect

119

Can Lauren

San José

On a secluded plot of land, surrounded by nature and a ten-minute drive from the beach, lies Can Lauren. Although the sea is close by, you cannot see it from here, but the wilderness around the house more than makes up for that. When you look at the villa, you immediately notice that this is not your typical Ibiza style, but more Moroccan kasbah. The inside, however, is typically Ibizan: a lot of white, and the distinctive room division and thick walls. The exterior terracotta-coloured walls were inspired by a Moroccan kasbah, no doubt due to the architect of this house having lived in Casablanca for years. In contrast, the rattan furniture around the swimming pool and in some sitting areas is Spanish and combines with some seventies touches left and right lending an eclectic air to it. The petanque court also gives away the current owners' origins!

The interior is whiter than white, with custom-made cabinets and furniture that is a motley collection of different styles and elements. Vintage furniture, Moroccan Berber rugs, modern pieces, and African objects make quite an interesting combination. The seventies make a comeback in the lamps, hairy-wool cushions, and glass side table.

The house is subdivided into two parts: the inhabitants use the ground floor's four bedrooms and two adjoining bathrooms, while the basement floor has a guest area with a master bedroom, adjoining living room, bathroom, and spacious terrace.

Vintage furniture, Moroccan Berber
rugs, modern pieces, and African
objects make quite an interesting
combination.

Can Trucci

Cap Martinet

HOUSES

The architect for this project, Belgian Bruno Erpicum, designed a timeless glass construction that, although it was built years ago, still looks contemporary. Because of the sloping terrain, which made constructing a house on this plot of land anything but self-evident, Bruno and his building experience in Ibiza were called upon. Nature takes precedence and influenced the volumes and the composition of the house. For this reason, the sleeping quarters are located on the ground floor, which has no direct line of sight to the sea, and the living areas are on top, resulting in a sweeping view of the Mediterranean. If you look really well, you can even see the vague outlines of Formentera and the city of Ibiza on the horizon.

The use of shutters and natural ventilation keeps the four rooms on the ground floor cool, while on hot days the first floor is cooled by opening the windows and letting a breeze provide relief from the heat. Decoration is very minimalist and the storage systems were carefully and discreetly worked into the interior. In the bedroom we recognize an Egg Chair by Arne Jacobsen, and six of his Swan Chairs sit around the dining table. The table itself is a Bonaldo design called Big Dining Table. The television corner has two Le Corbusier LC2 Chairs, and the living room an Eames Lounge Chair.

The swimming pool, which was oriented lengthwise to the south, has no borders. The water surface reflects the light and the sense of infinity makes you feel like you're swimming in the sea. If you want to dwell in a glass box like that, you have to accept that your life takes place in full view of the world, and more so at night, when Ibiza wakes up.

← Nature takes
precedence and influenced the
volumes and the composition of
the house.

The living areas are on top,
resulting in a sweeping view of the
Mediterranean.

← The swimming pool has no borders.
The water surface reflects the light
and the sense of infinity makes you
feel like you're swimming in the sea.

Charlotte de Lantsheere

CERAMICS

I-D

--------------------- Age: 41 years
--------------------- Has been living in Ibiza since 2013.
--------------------- Lives in San Mateo.
--------------------- Instagram: @charlotte_ceramics

PEOPLE

What's your story? How did you end up in Ibiza? —— Ibiza had been our fixed holiday destination for the last 17 years, it had become part of our lives, and we were really being drawn in by it. My husband, Eric Ceccarini, is a photographer and would often come to Ibiza for his fashion shoots because the light here is really wonderful. One day we simply made a decision to uproot and leave with our six-year-old daughter. She has totally adapted and is going to the village school, where she is very happy. As for me, I decided to keep busy making ceramics that I sell on the island. Business is going well.

What is it about the island that attracts you most? —— That's a no-brainer: the freedom! You can totally be yourself, you don't have to put on any kind of mask, or feel obliged to be a cog in someone else's wheel. I'm also hugely attracted by the diversity: so many different types of people and styles.

How do you fill in your days? —— In the morning we get up around eight, and I take my daughter to school. The following hours I spend in my workshop finishing orders or designing new creations. Around two I fetch my daughter from school and we set time aside for ourselves and our family. Then we go to the beach or to see friends. We go to bed around midnight. It is like this the whole year round and we're very happy with this way of life.

What is your favourite spot in Ibiza? —— Cala Xuclar is one of my favourites; it's not far from our home, and it's small and charming. There's also a small food place where you can have something to eat and drink. Es Portitxol is another fine place, a beach without too many people, surrounded by rocks and caves. You can't reach it by car and have to walk for fifteen minutes, so that helps to keep its charm alive. On Sunday we like to go to the hippy market in San Joan.

Where would you be living if Ibiza didn't exist? —— If Ibiza didn't exist, I'd be living in California or around Lisbon in Portugal.

---------------------- Tropical green garden wilderness
---------------------- Living area with an open fireplace
---------------------- Retro-inspired interior
---------------------- Situated in the old city of Ibiza

143

Casa Dalt Vila

Dalt Vila

Tucked away in one of the narrow streets of Ibiza Dalt Vila (the old city centre) lies this green paradise. A house that beguiles not through extreme luxury but with its charm, hanging gardens, and unlikely location for a holiday home: the city centre.
The house was originally divided into two separate floors, but the part above the living room was sacrificed to make more space and to allow outside light to flood the room. The presence of the big fireplace in the living area creates a sense of grandeur, making this house a cosy place to be in winter.

Through the clever use of contrasts, the owners succeeded in giving the interior character. The French empire-style chandelier contrasts with the imposing elongated sculptured Indonesian planter, while different hand-embroidered Afghan cushions add a lively touch to the classic white cotton chairs. In the bedroom, classic furniture mixes with an ethnic plaid and ditto wall covering.
Green plants almost throw themselves down from the ceiling ledges, creating the impression that the garden flows over into the interior of the house. The

lush garden is a carefully orchestrated chaos of pot plants, hanging plants, and flowers. Against the wall stand a wooden bench and a few small, low tables where you can sit every day to relax and enjoy the flora and fauna.

WALASSE TING

The lush garden is a carefully orchestrated chaos of pot plants, hanging plants, and flowers.

→ Casa Dalt Vila beguiles not through extreme luxury but with its charm, hanging gardens, and unlikely location for a holiday home: the city centre.

↓ Through the clever use of contrasts, the owners succeeded in giving the interior character.

→ The French empire-style chandelier contrasts with the imposing elongated sculptured Indonesian planter, while different hand-embroidered Afghan cushions add a lively touch to the classic white cotton chairs.

Geoffroy Gillieaux

FASHION DESIGNER
SHOP OWNER

I-D
-------------------- Age: 48 years
-------------------- Has been living in Ibiza for six years.
-------------------- Lives in San Mateo.
-------------------- Instagram: @jeffreysibiza

PEOPLE

What's your story? How did you end up in Ibiza? —— It was never my intention to move to Ibiza, but I was on holiday at a friend's here once who asked why I didn't move here. I thought it was a wonderful idea and checked with my employer at the time, *ELLE* magazine, to see if it was an option. As I was working for their website, it was, and so my boyfriend and I came over. I also opened a shop and combined both jobs. Through a friend I found a caretaker's house where the owners let me live in exchange for guarding and maintaining their property.

What is it about the island that attracts you most? —— The freedom! It's simply amazing how much freedom you have here. You come and go as you please, pursue any and all of your dreams, wear any clothes you want (no clothes is also an option, naturally), and be your real self.

How do you fill in your days? —— My life in Ibiza is divided into two halves: winter and summer. During the summer months my daily life consists of working, working, and working. During winter my retreat starts and I can enjoy life. It makes for a nice balance. In winter we live the way people used to live a hundred years ago, the real slow life. We get up at eight and have breakfast outside with fresh ingredients. We then work in the garden and I work on my collection, which has to be ready by spring. I also make many things myself; it's very labour intensive.

What is your favourite spot in Ibiza? —— My absolute favourite spot on the island is a small beach near the old city that nobody knows. Los Molinos is behind the citadel, you even have to drive through a small tunnel and go down some stairs and then you come to this kind of private beach that is hardly 50 metres wide that is usually as good as deserted. In winter you're also totally sheltered from the wind, so it really is ideal.

Where would you be living if Ibiza didn't exist? —— If I didn't live in Ibiza, I would've ended up in India or Indonesia, I think.

Paris 8 Juillet 98

Jeffrey's

Tina Cutler

HEALING PRACTITIONER

I-D

--------------------- Age: 51 years

--------------------- Has been living in Ibiza for 51 years.

--------------------- Lives in San Agustín.

--------------------- Instagram: @tinacutlerheals

What's your story? How did you end up in Ibiza? —— My parents came to Ibiza in the sixties and felt such a strong attraction to the island that they bought a house here. This is how I came to spend my childhood alternating between Ibiza and England, and have never known anything else. A few years back I was even a sort of socialite on the island who knew everything and everyone; I could arrange anything for anyone. They used to jokingly call me 'the queen of Ibiza'. Three years ago I put an end to my jet-set life and became a healer, a job that I split between London and Ibiza.

What is it about the island that attracts you most? —— Ibiza is my soul and my home. Its soil has fed me for the last 51 years, and I can't go without it. I have to admit it's become busier lately and I avoid the place during the busy periods. Its nature heals me: the trees, the beaches, the sun, the whole universe. Growing up here, we didn't have computers or iPads; we just played, and the natural and simple things we found lying about became toys. It was nice here on our little island, cut off from the world.

How do you fill in your days? —— During the periods of the year I spend in Ibiza, I usually wake up at five in the morning to meditate. Then I have breakfast, check my emails, and start working. I also like to take a lot of walks in between. I have been known to go down to the beach at noon to have lunch with friends. You know, in Ibiza you're allowed to just hang out, without any purpose, and to just enjoy yourself. I used to work very hard, and now I consciously take it easier.

What is your favourite spot in Ibiza? —— That's a secret I will never tell. Another nice spot is Sunset Ashram, cliché and many tourists, but I still find it magical to sit there and watch the sun go down over a drink.

Where would you be living if Ibiza didn't exist? —— I would in all likelihood be living in Africa, in Kenya! It's not the answer you were expecting but I think that living there would also be cool!

--------------------- Traditional *finca*
--------------------- Hand-made furnishings
--------------------- Peace and quiet
--------------------- Serene countryside setting

163

Can Basso

Santa Eulalia area

This more than 300-year-old *finca* is officially classified as a *finca agricola*. Now you need to know that for a building to receive this classification, it has to meet certain very specific requirements. Francis and Anne Dimmers, the promoters of this renovation project and Ibiza lovers through and through, wanted this classification and centred their renovation around it. The first requirement is that the building's facade and front door be oriented toward the south to ensure optimal temperature regulation inside. The front door cannot just be any front door, either: it has to have certain dimensions that are adapted to the inhabitants of Ibiza (who are clearly not very tall people).

The second tradition involves there being several spaces inside where olives or other crops can be stored, and a room without a ceiling where herbs can be dried. The third and last requirement has to do with rain water: the roof has to be flat and with small edges so that the rain water can be collected in a cistern (in Spanish: *el aljub*).

Francis started renovating in 2010 and asked furniture maker Thierry Billaud to make new doors and furniture yet as authentic as possible. The interior architects of Box 3 selected the right decorative elements and furniture items for the interior—Agape wash basins and Vola taps in the bathroom, and lamps by Tom Dixton and Ingo Maurer—as well as some vintage pieces like the 1956 Pierre Gautier Delaye chairs. A splendid holiday home for the Francis family!

↓ The interior architects of Box 3
selected the right decorative elements
and furniture items for the interior.

This more than 300-year-old *finca* is
officially classified as a *finca agricola*.

169

Can Cala Salada

Cala Salada

HOUSES

This project was carried out by architect Jordi Carreño and landscaped by designer Joan Macedo. The atypical Spanish interior has been done by Luis Laplace & Co who made it into a summer/winter house. Even in winter you will feel like you're in a summer house, and in summertime you will never be overwhelmed by the feeling that this is a winter house.
The house was built on a cliff overlooking the Mediterranean Sea. As the house looks like it is partly built into the rocks, its modern construction style does not clash with the brownish tints of the rocks and surrounding nature.
The house's three levels are connected with a lift. The ground level contains two suites that can be converted into separate, detached living spaces/living rooms. The intermediate level houses a unique terrace as well as a living room, kitchen, and dining room. The upper level has the master bedroom towering over it all, with an adjacent bathroom furnished in Arni Fantastico marble from Italy, a dressing room, study, restroom, and a second bedroom.
The stairs and paths surrounding the house entice you to go down and take an architectural stroll around the house.
The interior is lifted to a whole new level by the Velca Legnano armchairs and the Shell Chair by Hans J. Wegner for Fritz Hansen. The George Nakashima coffee table provides the space and warmth it needs. The floor lamp by designer Pierre Guariche adds a touch of red, which makes the whole area that much livelier and sparkling.
The swimming pool is surrounded by classic accessories such as the 1966 Richard Schultz for Knoll chaise lounge collection and the Butterfly BKF. The dining table outside has chairs by Richard Schultz for Knoll around it and nearby an Andrés Tallon wooden table.

The atypical Spanish interior has
been done by Luis Laplace & Co who
made it into a summer/winter house.

175

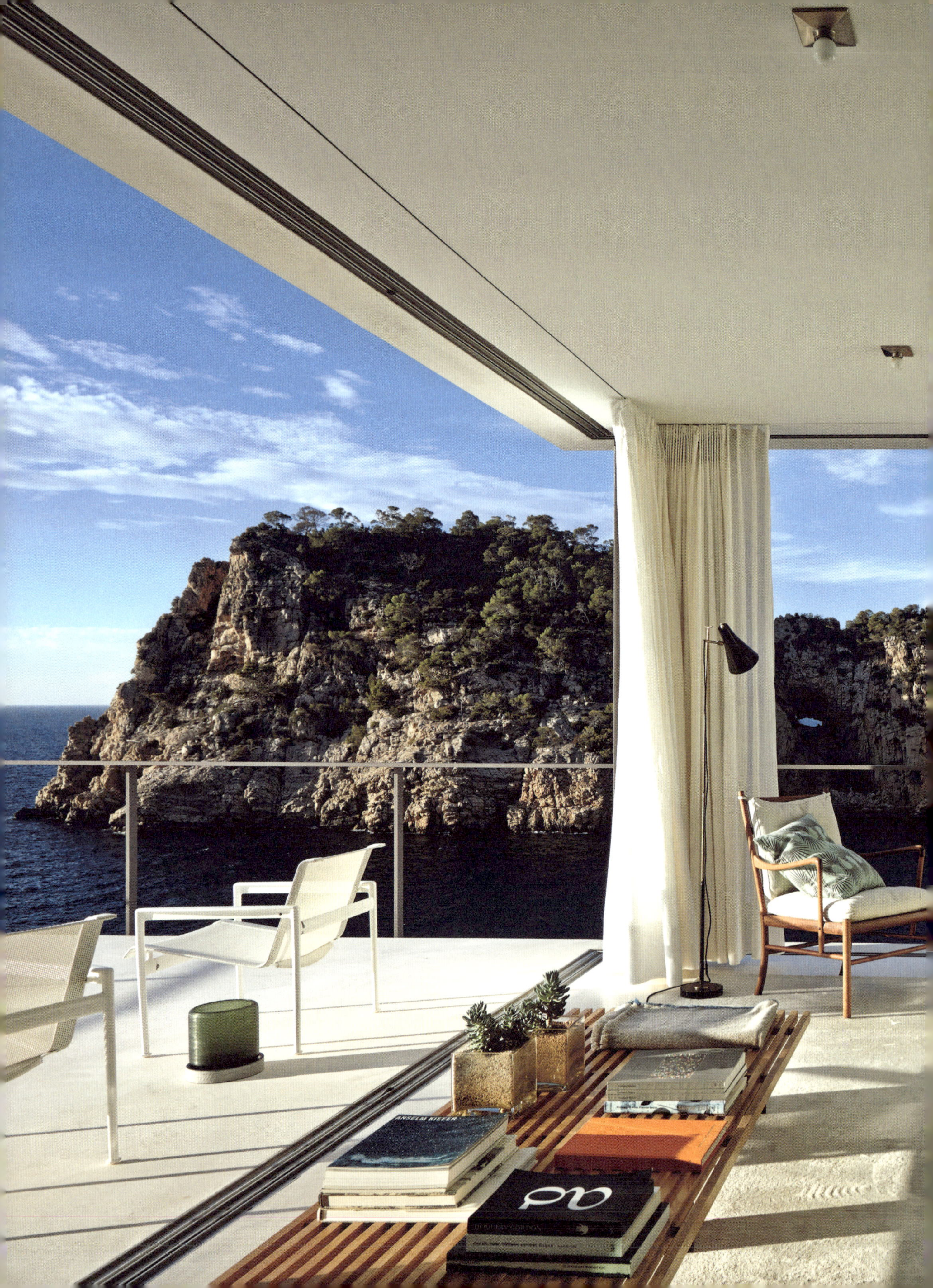
ANSELM KIEFER

↓ As the house looks like it is partly built into the rocks, its modern construction style does not clash with the brownish tints of the rocks and surrounding nature.

179

Carmen Straatsma

INTERIOR DESIGNER

I-D
-------------------- Age: 39 years
-------------------- Has been living on Ibiza since 2008.
-------------------- Lives in San Mateo.
-------------------- Instagram: @carmenstraatsma

PEOPLE

What's your story? How did you end up in Ibiza? ——— After a close friend of mine bought a small house in the countryside, I went to visit him for a week. I'd known Ibiza mostly for its nightlife, but during that week I fell in love twice. First with the friend, and then with the island. We started doing the house up together and for eight years we travelled back and forth between Amsterdam and Ibiza until we decided to live in Ibiza permanently. I'd just given birth to my second child and started to enjoy city life less and less. I wanted to see the children grow up in a more free and natural environment and Ibiza was the ideal place for that, and still is. I was editor in chief at *Elle Girl* magazine, but gave up my job without thinking twice. The first few years I enjoyed doing nothing. Well, I read a lot, got my driver's license and started decorating my house passionately. That eventually lead to a new career and business.

What is it about the island that attracts you most? ——— The freedom, and a sense of peacefulness, not always apparent in summer. It's also important for me to be in touch with nature and experience the changes of rhythm that are so typical here. Personally I find it easier to really be myself here than anywhere else. There is a unbeatable quality of acceptance to the island, and I have the feeling it encourages and sometimes even pushes you to find your own way. That in combination with a lot of likeminded, non-judgemental people living here makes it the perfect place. I sometimes miss the creative buzz of the city and I often wonder how much more work I'd be able to do without the slow pace and distractions you have here, but to be completely honest, it's worth it.

How do your fill your days? ——— Weekdays start at half past seven, after which I take my children to school. Work is different every day. There are times I'm frantically driving around the island, spending days on building sites or moving furniture around, but I also have a studio in the village of Santa Gertrudis and days there more resemble the office life I was used to. Everything takes ages here to get done in the right way, so it's never boring. I still love going to the beach with the children—the typical holiday life is still part of our routine and I feel very privileged to be able to enjoy it, but we also spend quite some time in Santa Gertrudis after school, where they have a lot of friends to play with and our favourite little *gelateria*.

What is your favourite spot in Ibiza? ——— It's a real cliché, but I guess you don't want to hear that, do you? If I have to choose a place that's not home, I'd pick the cliffs close to Cala Xuclar. It's a little hideaway for the kids and I. We jump of the rocks and go on long swimming adventures. I used to live more in the south of Ibiza, but since moving further north that area has really stolen my heart. San Mateo, Santa Agnes, San Miguel, … are still so authentic. But for me the best restaurant is still on the other side. I love Can Domingo near San Jose, on summer nights this is definitely my favourite spot.

Where would you be living if Ibiza didn't exist? ——— I haven't found a place where I feel more at home yet, but I sometimes see myself living in Morocco. It's very different from Ibiza, where I can relate more to the culture and lifestyle, but I had that same sense of falling in love with a place there. So maybe someday … but not until I'm really old!

Melanie Ireland

STYLIST AND FOUNDER OF KID'S FASHION BRAND SIMPLE KIDS

I-D
-------------------- ———— Age: 51 years
-------------------- ———— Has been coming to Ibiza for 30 years.
-------------------- ———— Lives in Cala Vadella.
-------------------- ———— Instagram: @casamelibiza

What's your story? How did you end up in Ibiza? ———— The very first time I came to Ibiza was with a friend who had to do a lot of convincing to get me to set foot ashore. When I arrived, I had an instant feeling that this was love. An immediate love affair with the island. I had immediate visions of living here, going to the market with my basket, and living on the beach. I am not actually a permanent resident here—I go back and forth between Belgium and Ibiza—but I certainly want to settle here permanently sometime in the future. First, though, I want my kids to fly the nest in Belgium. They're eighteen and twenty now so the big step is not that far off!

What is it about the island that attracts you most? ———— The light! I don't have to think about it for more than a second. The light's impact on the colours. Green becomes intense green in Ibiza. Blue becomes almost transparent in this place. Everything is more intense. Also the vibe that's in the air, and nature, which is incredibly unique and beautiful. This is the only place on earth where I can slow down, forget about things, and literally rest. I also find Ibiza to be a feminine island; its energy suits women. My new collection LEA is also to a large extent inspired by Ibiza; I couldn't find any long dresses that weren't transparent anywhere, so I started my own collection. Dresses I can wear non-stop when I am in Ibiza.

How do you fill in your days? ———— I always wake up earlier than I want to in Ibiza. I feel it's because of the rock of Es Vedra. You see, it's right in front of my flat and it's full of minerals that emit this energetic power. It may sound strange, but I feel this energy here in my home. The first thing I do when I get up is sit on my terrace, have a cup of coffee, and look at Es Vedra. After which life gets off to a very slow start. I walk to the beach, to a small bar where they know me and I can have a nice breakfast. Then I go shopping in the local supermarket and think really hard about which beach I am going to visit that day! The slow life, isn't it wonderful. I eat lunch very late in the afternoon, and I love to linger at the table. This way I don't need to have dinner anymore and I can go to bed early, around ten or so. What I like the most is coming to Ibiza with my daughters.

What is your favourite spot in Ibiza? ———— Es Vedra is my absolute number one. But I also love Es Cavallet, not the popular part at El Chiringuito, but when you continue walking in the direction of the lighthouse. At that stretch of beach, the water is a clear blue and super soft. I really go there for the incredible water. Did you know, by the way, that the water in Ibiza is of exceptionally good quality and among one of the finest in the world? The deeper you go into the water, the better for your health.

Where would you be living if Ibiza didn't exist? ———— Tulum is my second Ibiza, although it's got too crowded over the last few years.

Can Caterina

Santa Gertrudis

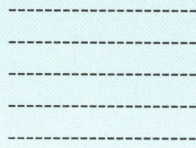

Calm Scandinavian style
with baby blue, wood, and nature
Private nature trail
Space & air for free
Into-the-wild setting

This breath-taking, timeless *finca*, constructed and furnished by architect Cate Watts, pops up in the hills around the small village of Santa Gertrudis. Its 70,000 square metres of surrounding estate make you feel alone on the island, even though you are just a stone's throw from the charming village centre and its cosy little restaurants and shops.

No neighbours looking in, and grand views of the island and its natural environment ... Starting and finishing your day with the sun. Its Scandinavian-borrowed style, finished with Eames seating and mod wicker furnishings, inspires guests to return to nature, helped along by the furry throws, wicker elements, and rough wood accents.
The flowers in the garden lend the whole an extra touch of colour.
The swimming pool is surrounded by lavender fences.

↓ The Scandinavian-borrowed style of the house inspires guests to return to nature.

Victoria Durrer

DESIGNER AND SHOP OWNER

I-D
-------------------- Age: 57 years
-------------------- Has been living in Ibiza for 23 years.
-------------------- Lives in Santa Agnes.
-------------------- Instagram: @lagaleriaelefante

What's your story? How did you end up in Ibiza? —— My parents were fervent sailors and were already coming here by boat in the sixties. Of course, back in those days the island was still pretty much deserted and totally unknown. Hippies were just beginning to move here. Then, in the sixties, they decided to buy a house here. So I've been coming to Ibiza from a very early age and it's really my home. Twenty-three years ago I moved here with my husband and our son, as I wanted him to grow up outdoors, playing outside in nature. I'm a textile designer, and I love to paint. I started making accessories that I would sell locally and to friends. This led me to the opening of my first shop at La Paloma, and then later La Galeria Elefante. We've always travelled and we love to go to hidden corners on a mission to source beautiful things for my shops.

What is it about the island that attracts you most? —— My answer is probably the same as everyone's: the light, the landscape and the sea. During the summer months we go out on our fishing boat every day, mostly to small islands in the west to swim, picnic, and to watch sunsets. We prefer sailing to the north and west: the north because it's quieter there and the west because that's where the sun sets.

How do you fill in your days? —— I tend to get up early and start with yoga, and then a long walk with my dog. If it's summer I always go for an early swim around 8.30 AM for an hour and then play my day, either whilst swimming or whilst walking. Mostly I need to go to either of the shops, La Paloma or La Galeria Elefante, and invariably I have appointments. Otherwise I work from my studio at home. There's often a social moment in the day, and then most afternoons we go boating. My house is in the summer often full of friends, so there's a lot of time spent on deciding on meals. We often go to La Paloma, as it's so relaxed and friendly. Then we go back home to chat and to listen to music.

What is your favourite spot in Ibiza? —— When there's a full moon, we often go for a walk on the cliffs and take a picnic and a guitar, or go on our boat to a secluded bay. Can Guimo is a great place to eat in the day as well as in the evening for a relaxed and local atmosphere. And I definitely love to eat at La Paloma, which is one of my favourite restaurants. You get a real feel of Ibiza, and the food is simply yummy! Cala Bonita is also one of my favourite spots to just sit on the rocks and stare out to sea.

Where would you be living if Ibiza didn't exist? —— Perhaps Marine county, north of San Francisco, or Madagascar, a total dream country. As we're a family of nomads, we could easily try something totally different!

Can Nou

San José

----------------------- Idyllic countryside location
----------------------- Secluded setting
----------------------- Family-focused wonderland
----------------------- Large landscaped gardens

209

HOUSES

Before architect Bruno Erpicum of the architectural firm AABE starts work on a project, he goes to the spot and takes time to read the landscape: observe, interpret, and convert into knowledge. In this case, he sees a house with different volumes which he connects with white walls and blocks.

To understand the layout you have to know that there is, on the one hand, a main building with the living spaces and master bedroom, and then there are two separate areas connected by walls. One of these separate volumes houses three rooms, while the other houses a bedroom. Guests can thus enjoy needed privacy and a relaxing view of the garden from their own bedroom.

In the big living area inside we find a modular chair designed by Antonio Citterio for Flexform. The stools are by Poliform and the coffee tables by Giuseppe Vigano for Longhi. The two armchairs are by Eames for Vitra. Connoisseurs will recognise the Fortuny lamp designed by Mariano Fortuny for Pallucco. In the background we see a large painting by artist Peter Terrin. The solid-wood Carpintería Pazos dining table stands in stark contrast to the easily recognisable Panton chairs by Verner Panton for Vitra. The chandelier in red Murano glass is by La Murrina.

Landscape architect Roger Meier was assigned this project and came over to divide the terrain into smaller plots with autochthonous Mediterranean plants, many of them aromatic. The most conspicuous ones are the blue flowers. The garden contains many small benches providing an opportunity to sit, watch, and meditate. Marés was used in the garden, a type of sandstone from the Balearic Islands that has a wonderful golden colour. The age-old olive trees welcome visitors to the garden.

The swimming pool, elegantly edged with polished Capri limestone, is discreetly hidden behind a stone wall. The loungers were custom made. The shady area next to the pool was turned into an exterior summer diner with a custom-made marble table and, once more, Panton chairs by Verner Panton for Vitra.

← The shady area next to the pool was turned into an exterior summer diner with a custom-made marble table and Panton chairs by Verner Panton for Vitra.

213

There is, on the one hand, a main building with the living spaces and master bedroom, and then there are two separate areas connected by walls. Guests can thus enjoy needed privacy and a relaxing view of the garden from their own bedroom.

Ibiza Treasures

Apart from fantastic houses, Ibiza has got a couple of secrets up its sleeve that will make your heart beat faster: marvellous sleeping accommodations, hidden beaches, and insane restaurants. You'll never want to leave the island again, guaranteed. Only the very best of the island, handpicked by yours truly.

TO SLEEP
OR NOT TO SLEEP?

Ibiza has loads of places where
you can spend the night: hotels,
flats, hostels, B&Bs, etc. It does
have many more high-quality
accommodation options on
agrotourism and rural hotels,
places that combine the splendour
of traditional architecture with
exceptional surroundings and
fields where fruit and vegetables
are grown.

PURE HOUSE IBIZA

If you think you know all of Ibiza's
hidden treasures, you are very much
mistaken. This 30-acre domain
contains a tropical garden lush with
exotic plants and olive trees, and
fincas furbished as luxurious, boho
sleeping quarters. Add to that the
warmth of its owners Caroline and
Rushan, and you couldn't wish for
anything more. Pure House gets its
electricity from solar panels and
only uses eco-friendly bath and
cleaning products. The fruit and
vegetables are home grown as much
as possible, and all other food comes
from local farmers and is organic.
Heaven is a little place on earth.
www.purehouseibiza.com
— *From €190*

LOS ENAMORADOS

This relatively new hotel, run by
former basketball player Pierre
and his wife Rosemarijn, lies in
an unspoiled spot up north. It is
something in between a hotel,
restaurant, shop, and bar. The
eclectic interior is a must-see and as
a guest you can even buy anything
you see, from vintage treasures to
carefully selected design objects
brought back by the owners from
the far ends of the world. You can
sleep in one of the nine rooms and
dine on the terrace, all with a view
of the sea. There is no swimming
pool, but you have the bright blue
sea right in front of you if you want
to go skinny dipping.
www.losenamoradosibiza.com
— *From €225*

LA GRANJA

Living in clover in Ibiza. This farm
mansion offers a unique sight: a
small-scale hotel with nine rooms,
a separate guesthouse with two
bedrooms, a swimming pool, and
a farmer's table where you can
savour the domain's most succulent
ingredients. La Granja embraces its
farmhouse heritage and connection
with the estate. Peace, simplicity,
and aesthetics aptly describe this
place.
www.lagranjaibiza.com
From €350

TO EAT
OR NOT TO EAT?

Your quest for culinary satisfaction ends here and now! Ibiza is very famous for its quintessential dining in combination with stunning sea views or cool countryside hangouts. Vegetarians are not excluded and detoxers are served by experts in nutrition.

The island's numerous restaurants, characterised by their extraordinary quality, offer fresh products, such as fish and seafood, or traditional dishes like *bullit de peix** or *sofrit pagès***. Some of its most outstanding desserts are the *flaó* (a delicious cake made with goat and sheep cheese, and peppermint) and *greixonera* (a pudding with an ensaimada base, milk, and egg).

*   A fish-based dish prepared in a pan.
**   An Ibizan dish of gently spiced pork, lamb, and chicken, with gorgeous local *sobrasada* and *butifarra* sausage, whole sweet garlics, peppers, and potatoes.

CALA BONITA

One of Ibiza's most popular and special spots is without a doubt the idyllic Cala Bonita. A basic little beach that has loungers, few tourists, and a restaurant nearby where chef Pau Barba does his all to offer patrons some of the island's most authentic flavours. The restaurant also has a more informal section, Tapas Bonitas, where you don't need to make a reservation. You can just walk in, sit down, order some tapas (small dishes), and wash them down with a nice cocktail or glass of wine.
www.calabonitaibiza.com

CAN DOMO

Although its location among the hills around Santa Eulalia keeps it out of sight, Can Domo can hardly be called a 'hidden' pearl. This agrotourism hotel received several extensions over the years, one of which was a full-fledged restaurant headed by chef Pau Barba. Barba's prior experience in high-end cuisine allows him to put a modern twist on traditional Catalan dishes. Unforgettable flavours in an amazing setting, with tranquillity and distance views included.
www.candomo.com

LA LUNA NELL' ORTO

In the seventies this place was the venue for one of the first hippy markets, and the atmosphere from those days still floats in the air. The handmade benches, brickwork tables, and old fig trees all hark back to Ibiza's original *fincas*. Located in one of the island's most privileged spots, the village of San Miguel, this restaurant is a must visit. The evenings here are so peaceful and quiet, under the old fig tree, the light of the sun reflecting on the whitewashed rustic houses decorating this picturesque rural village. La Luna Nell'Orto is one of those places that let you explore Ibiza in a pleasant, peaceable way.

www.lunanellorto.com

LAMUELLA

Right in the heart of the north lies Lamuella, to many people one of Ibiza's finest eating establishments. In 2016, sweethearts Illan and Shiran Dascal landed on the white island and started their own restaurant and lifestyle concept centred around food, style, music, art, and dance. While Lamuella's core business is the restaurant with its Mediterranean/Asian cuisine, you just have to check out the adjacent shop, too! Its collection of items on sale, carefully selected by the owners in India, is unique on the island. To top it all off, there is a cosy club, a kids' area, and an art gallery.

www.lamuella-ibiza.eltenedor.rest

LA PALOMA

La Paloma restaurant has made a name for itself on the island as the place to go to when you want a break from the hustle and bustle. Although ... you will find it packed every day, and rightly so. The menu features wholesome Mediterranean/Italian dishes lovingly prepared with respect for tradition as well as homemade cocktails that will lift you to higher realms. The restaurant's atmosphere is boho chic: wooden tables, lampions, and orange trees. Fashion designer Valentino and model Kate Moss have been known to dine there incognito.

www.palomaibiza.com

LOS PATIOS

Los Patios is the name of the universe created by entrepreneur David Leppan. And like the universe, his vision is grand: several restaurants, a bakery, a wellness space, a shop, an exhibition space, big terraces, and a wonderful tropical garden. Everything is prepared with local products, home-grown produce, and organic ingredients. A must-see when you're in Ibiza.

www.lospatiosibiza.com

SECRET BEACHES

Not only the restaurants and clubs fill to the brim during the island's high season; most beaches are packed, too. You can still find peaceful spots away from the madness, though. Try some of these hidden gems:

CALA ESCONDIDA

Hidden between the rocks of one of Ibiza's most touristic spots—Sunset Ashram—lies this little beach, one that should, in fact, be kept secret from tourists, for you can still enjoy it in relative peace. As you can the beach bar, which offers a splendid view of the island's most impressive natural phenomenon, its famed sunsets. Once the dying sun's last rays caress the pink rocks, an unlikely glow emerges. A glow that invites you to sit down and savour the moment with a sip of wine. A true spectacle.

HOW TO GET THERE?

→   Park your car and walk for two minutes. Drive to Sunset Ashram and park your car on the side of the road or in the car park. When looking out to sea with Sunset Ashram in front of you, Cala Escondida is on the far left. Walk over the rocks until you reach the coastline and you will see some steps that take you down to the beach.

CALA LLENTRISCA

For this beach, located in a popular area of the island, to have remained so unknown is actually quite surprising. The first thing you notice when coming upon it is how blue the water is. So blue, in fact, that it almost hurts to look at. Cala Llentrisca is a place you go to when you want to relax looking at fishing boats bobbing up and down, far out to sea. The jetty allows you to enter and leave the water without hurting your feet; quite a luxury! Another plus: you can soak up the sun's rays until late in the afternoon, which you cannot do in the east and south of the island! Hello sunset aperitif!

HOW TO GET THERE?

→   Drive to the centre of Es Cubells. After the speed bumps, turn left (before the church) and follow the road to Cala Llentrisca for four kilometres. Take a right at the fork after three kilometres. Follow the road until it stops and leave your car, making sure that it does not block traffic. A small path leads you down to the beach in about ten minutes.

ES PORTITXOL

This small beach is located between cliffs whose shape transform it into a natural harbour with crystal-clear azure water. To reach it, you have to descend a dangerous, rickety path, which adds to the thrill of the location. Once down at the beach, you find yourself in a piece of paradise whose inaccessibility ensures you will be largely undisturbed. The local fishermen use it as a place to store their boats. The route you take down to the beach holds a lot of history: fishermen, pirates, and invaders have been using the same path for hundreds of years.

HOW TO GET THERE?

→   Set off from the centre of San Miguel to San Mateo. After about 1.5 kilometres, take a right at the fork to San Mateo Nord. Follow this road to Illa Blanca for three kilometres. Right before Illa Blanca, turn left and drive on down along an estate. When the road turns from asphalt to dust, leave your car. Continue down on foot for ten minutes, taking a left when you reach a fork. After a sharp turn to the right you will see a wall on the left and a small path ahead that leads you down to the beach through the wood.

Blakstad: p. 7, 38-39, 40-41
Serge Anton: p. 8-9, 42-43, 44, 118-125
Gypsy Westwood: p. 10, 12-13, 16, 18-19, 22-23, 45, 48, 50, 80-85, 104-109, 136-141, 150-161, 188-193, 204-207, 221 (bottom right)
Los Enamorados: p. 11, 219 (top right)
Shutterstock: p. 14-15, 28, 32-33, 223 (bottom)
Getty Images: p. 17, 26-27, 30-31, 34-35, 36-37
Aisha Bonet (www.aishabonet.com): p. 20-21
Toni Ramon: p. 24, 25
Jill Gillessen: p. 29
Fernando Alda: p. 46-47, 54-79
La Luna nell' Orto: p. 49, 221 (top left)
La Paloma: p. 51, p. 221 (bottom left)
Eugeni Pons: p. 52, 86-103, 172-181, 194-203, 208-217
Adrian Houston: p. 110-117
Laurent Brandajs: p. 126-135, 164-165, 166 (top), 167 (bottom)
Montse Garriga Grau: p. 142-149
Ibiza.be: p. 162, 166 (bottom), 168, 169
Karel Balas: p. 163, 170-171
Carmen Straatsma: p. 182-187
Pure House Ibiza: p. 219 (top left)
La Granja: p. 219 (bottom)
Cala Bonita: p. 220 (top)
Can Domo: p. 220 (bottom)
Lamuella: p. 221 (top right)
Los Patios: p. 221 (bottom right)
Cala Escondida: p. 222
Cala Llentrisca: p. 223 (top)

AUTHOR

Anne Poelmans

TRANSLATION

Xavier De Jonge

© Lannoo Publishers, 2018

D/2018/45/21 – NUR 450/500

ISBN: 978 94 014 4910 6

www.lannoo.com

If you have any questions or comments
about the material in this book, please
do not hesitate to contact our editorial
team: markedteam@lannoo.com

This book is
MARKED

MARKED is an initiative by
Lannoo Publishers.
www.marked-books.com

JOIN THE MARKED COMMUNITY
on @booksbymarked

Or sign up for our MARKED
newsletter with news about new
and forthcoming publications on
art, interior design, food & travel,
photography and fashion as well as
exclusive offers and MARKED events
on www.marked-books.com

#AREYOUMARKED